Unit 5
Workbook

This Workbook contains worksheets that accompany many of the lessons from the *Teacher Guide* for Unit 5. Each worksheet is identified by the lesson number in which it is used. The worksheets in this book do not include written instructions for students because the instructions would have words that are not decodable. Teachers will explain these worksheets to the students orally, using the instructions in the Teacher Guide. The Workbook is a student component, which means each student should have a Workbook.

Name _____

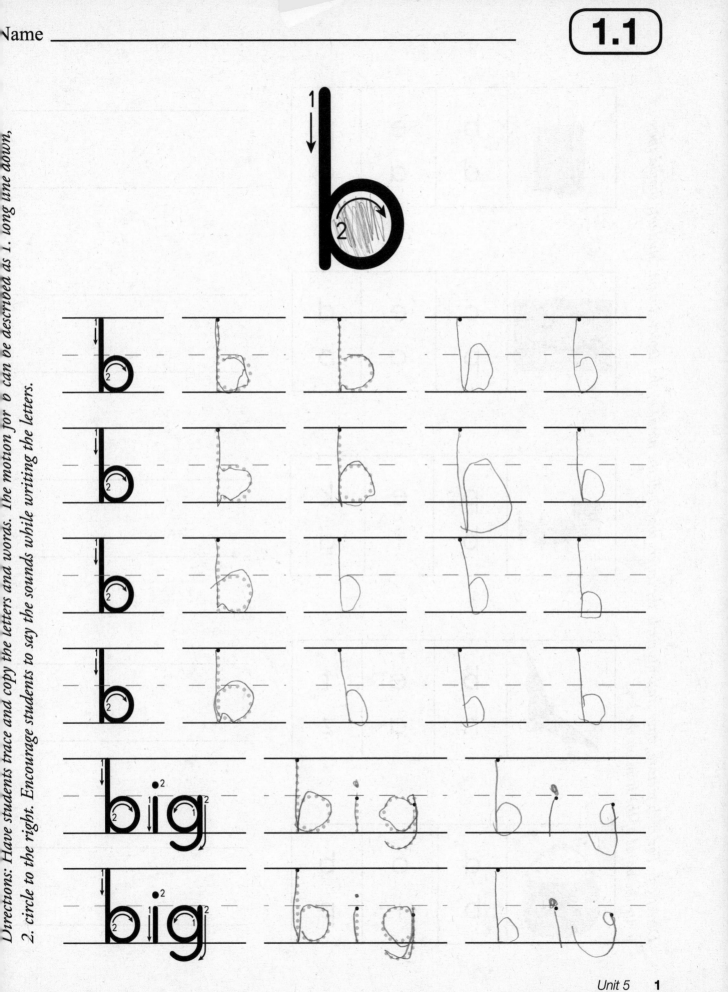

Directions: Have students trace and copy the letters and words. The motion for b can be described as 1. long line down, 2. circle to the right. Encourage students to say the sounds while writing the letters.

© 2013 Core Knowledge Foundation

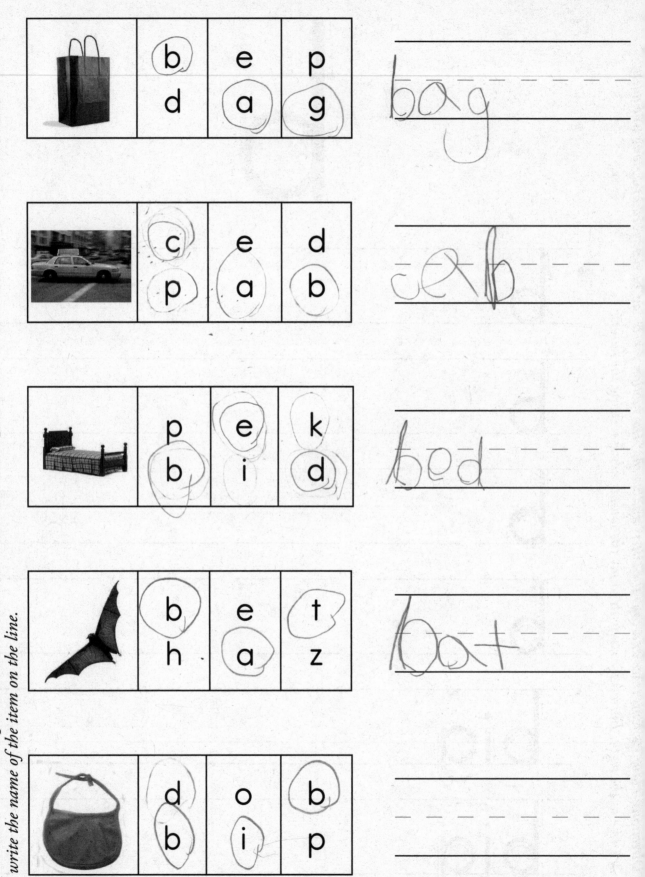

bag

ca b

bed

bat

Dear Family Member,

On the front and back of this worksheet, have your child draw a line from each word on the left to the matching picture. If necessary, identify the pictures for your child.

1. cab

2. bed

3. bag

4. cat

5. zip

6. pig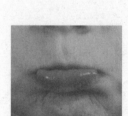

7. hat

8. van

9. sad

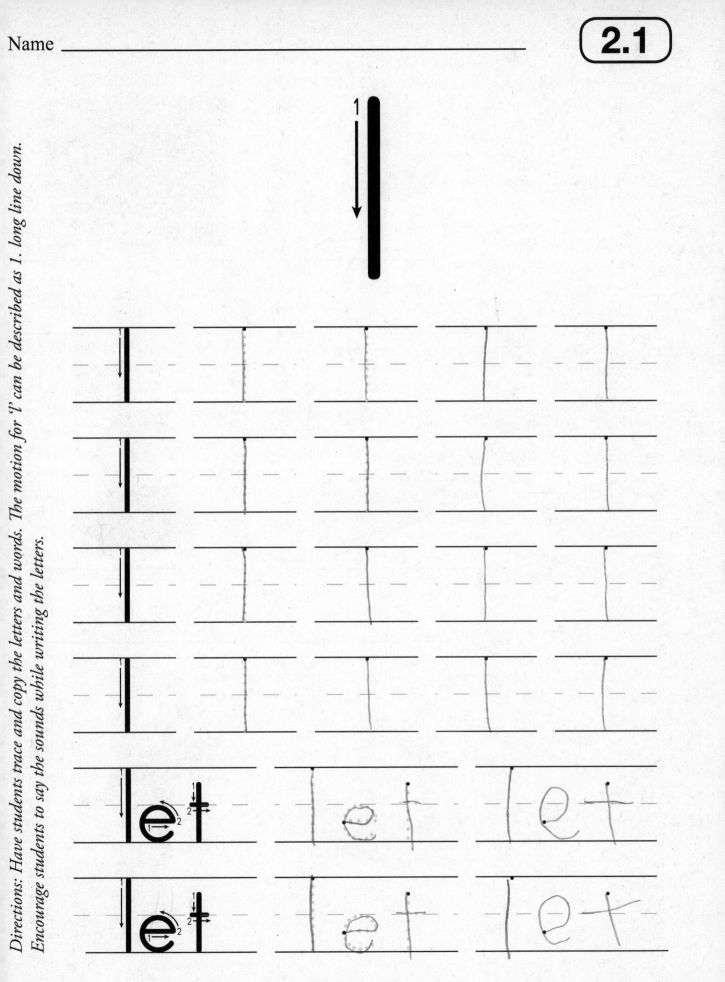

Directions: Have students trace and copy the letters and words. The motion for 'l' can be described as 1. long line down. Encourage students to say the sounds while writing the letters.

1. lip

2. log

3. leg

Directions: Have students trace and copy the letters and words. The motion for 'r' can be described as 1. short line down, 2. half a bump. Encourage students to say the sounds while writing the letters.

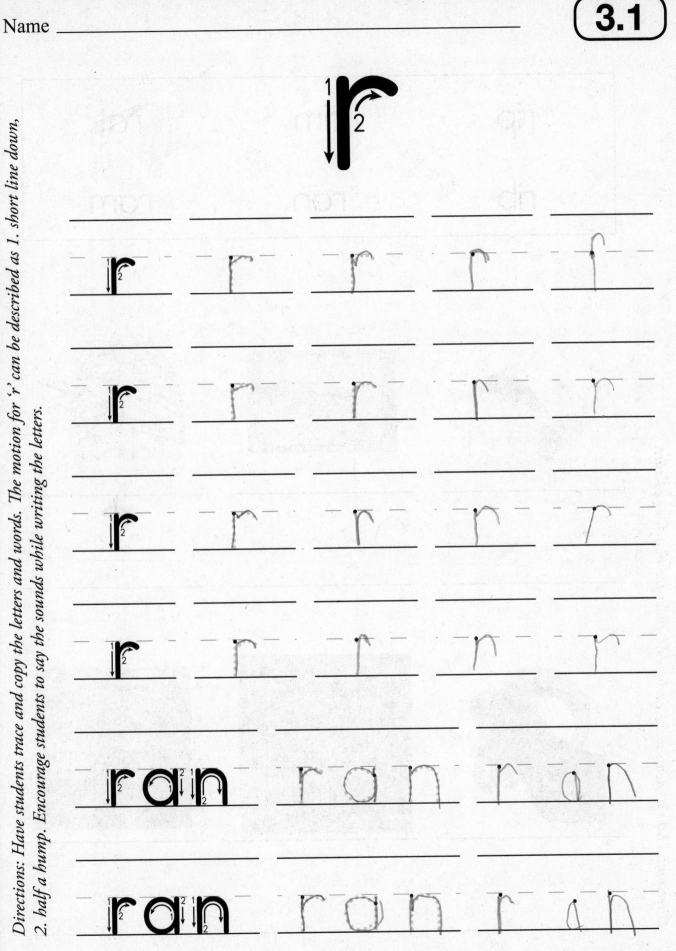

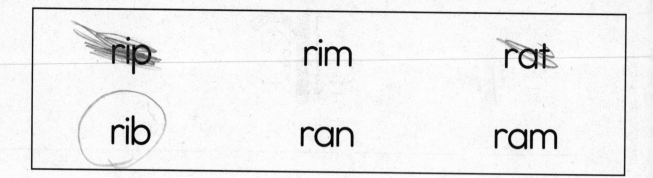

rip   rim   rat

rib   ran   ram

rat   rip   rib

rat

Directions: For each picture, have students circle the matching word.

1. let   leg   beg

2. bat   sag   bag

3. lot   log   hog

4. bib   bit   did

5. bet   bed   led

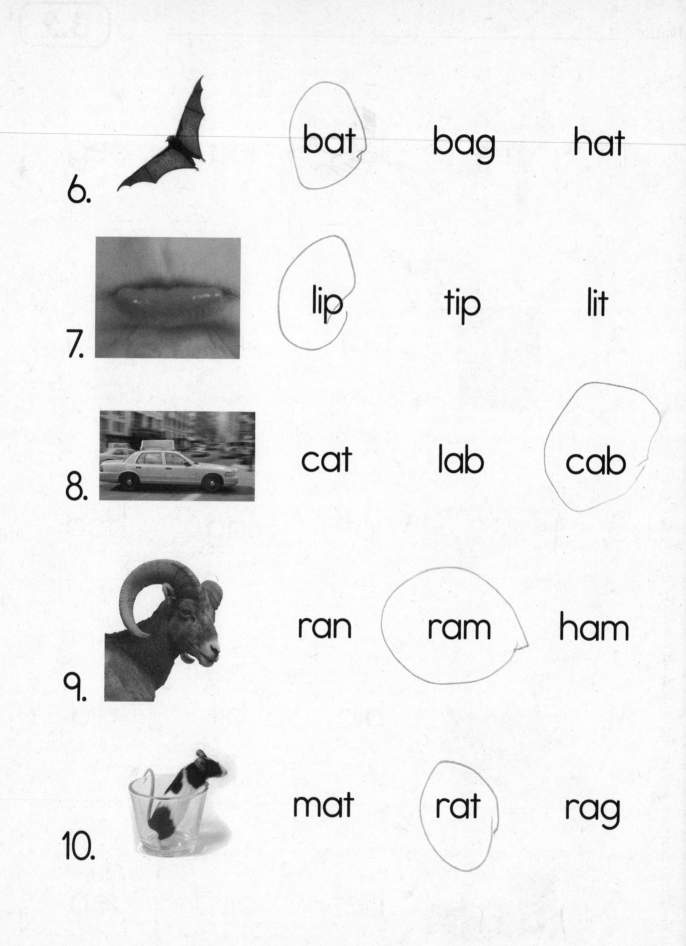

6. bat   bag   hat

7. lip   tip   lit

8. cat   lab   cab

9. ran   ram   ham

10. mat   rat   rag

Directions: Have students trace and copy the letters and words. The motion for 'u' can be described as 1. cup, 2. short line down. Encourage students to say the sounds while writing the letters.

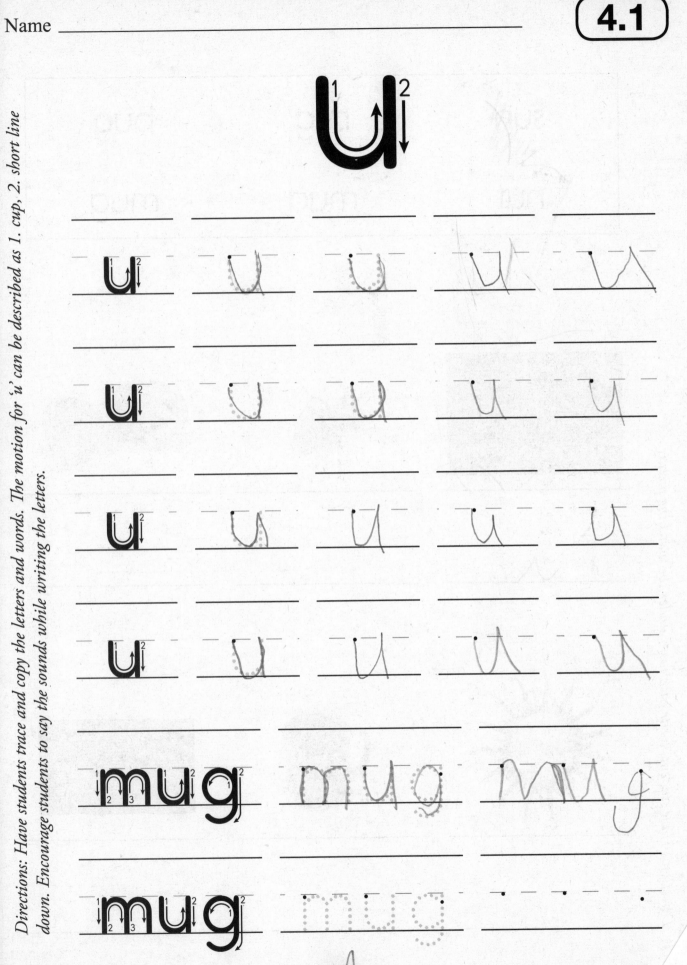

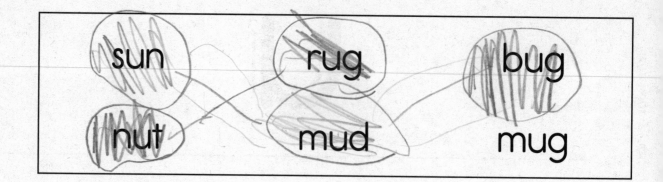

sun   rug   bug

nut   mud   mug

mud   bug   nut

Sun   mug   rug

Name _____

Dear Family Member,

Help your child cut out the two circles. Pin the smaller circle on top of the larger circle with a brass fastener. Ask your child to spin the smaller circle to make words. Have your child read the words he or she makes.

Handwriting Practice: Ask your child to copy the words on a sheet of paper.

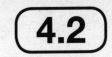

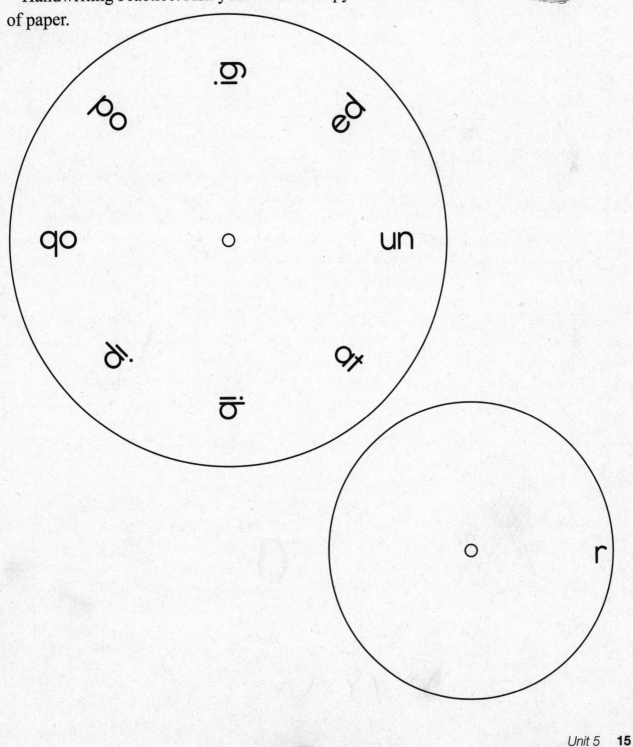

1. mud

Mud

2. leg

eg

Directions: Have students write each word under the matching picture.

3. rat

rat

4. rip

 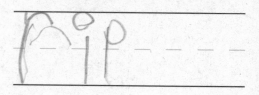

_____ _____
_____ _____

_____ _____
nip

5. nut

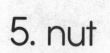 

_____ _____
nut

6. bat

_____ _____
bat

Name _____

1. lip

2. mug

3. ram

4. bug

5. bag

Directions: Draw a line from each word on the left to the matching picture.

6. leg

7. rat

8. log

9. bed

10. sun

Directions: Have students trace and copy the letters and words. The motion for 'w' can be described as 1. diagonal right, 2. diagonal up, 3. diagonal right, 4. diagonal up. Encourage students to say the sounds while writing the letters.

1. web

We b

2. wig

Wig

3. wet

Wet

Name _____

Dear Family Member,

   On the front and back of this worksheet, have your child copy each word under the matching picture. If necessary, identify and name the pictures for your child.

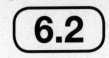

1. nut

nat

2. bat

bat

3. rip

rip

4. mud

5. web

6. run

Directions: Have students trace and copy the letters and words. The motion for 'j' can be described as 1. fish hook ending below bottom line, 2. dot on top. Encourage students to say the sounds while writing the letters.

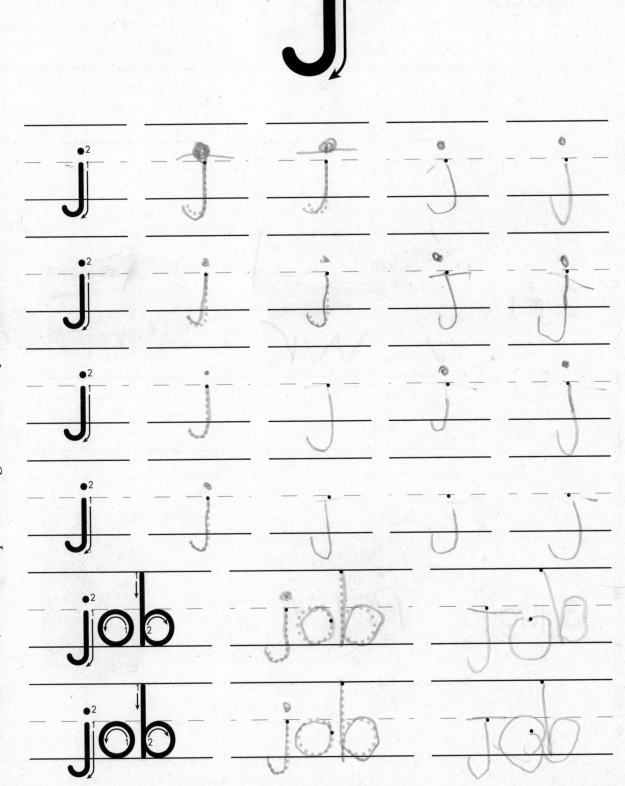

© 2013 Core Knowledge Foundation

1. jog

jog

2. jet

jet

3. jug

jug

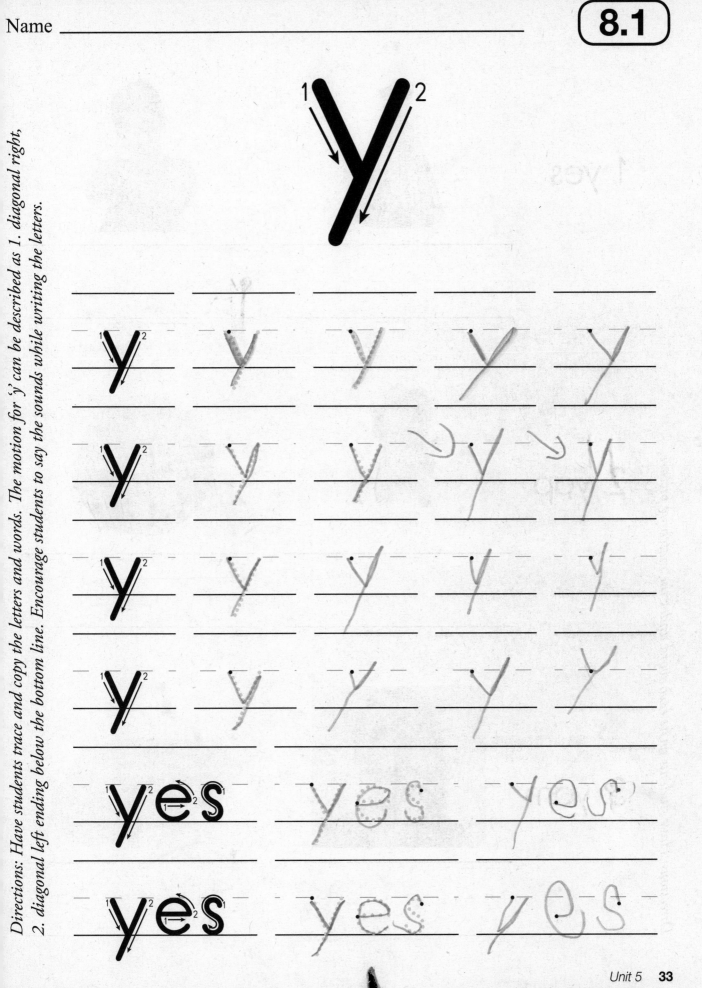

Directions: Have students trace and copy the letters and words. The motion for 'y' can be described as 1. diagonal right, 2. diagonal left ending below the bottom line. Encourage students to say the sounds while writing the letters.

1. yes

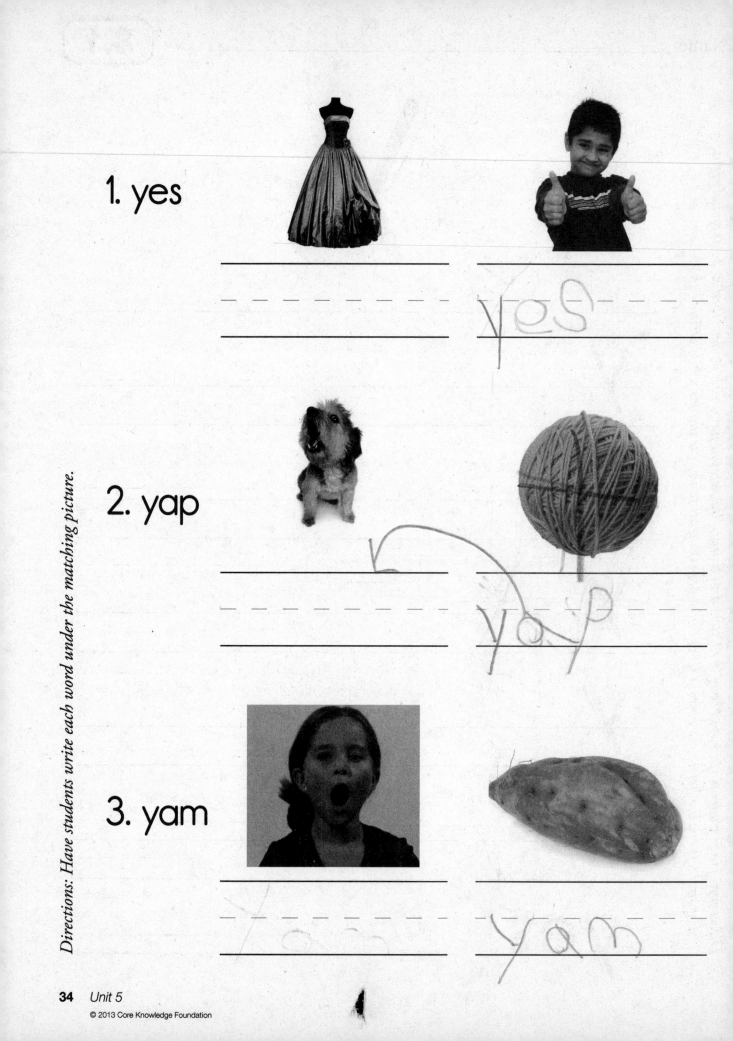

yes

2. yap

yap

3. yam

yam

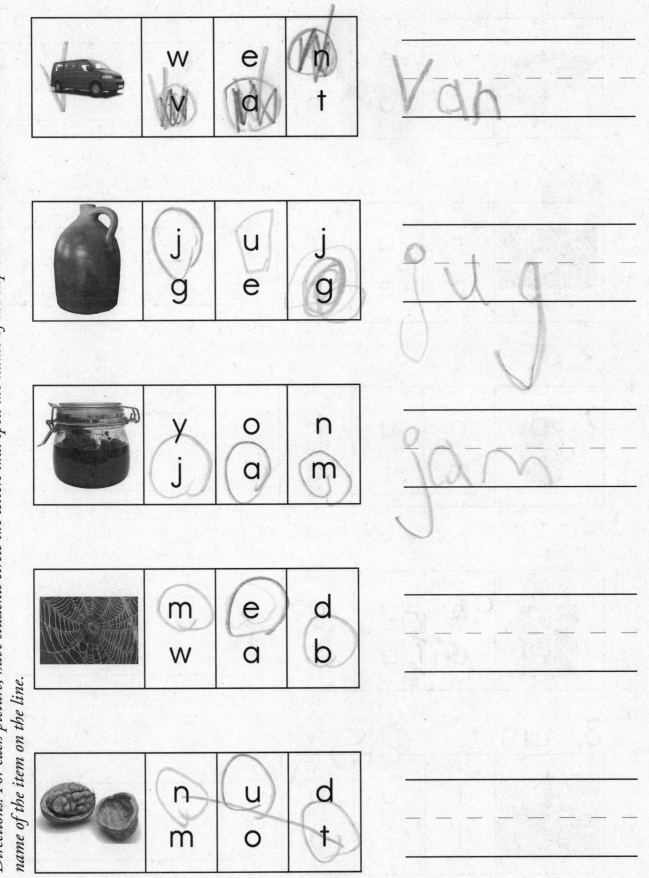

Directions: For each picture, have students circle the letters that spell the name of the depicted item. Students should write the name of the item on the line.

Van

jug

jam

	v / y	e / a	m / n	
				_____

	r / n	u / e	j / g	
				_____

	n / m	u / i	k / g	
				_____

	b / d	a / e	g / t	
				_____

	t / l	u / i	p / g	
				_____

1. jet

2. leg

Directions: Draw a line from each word on the left to the matching picture.

3. ram

4. nut

5. wig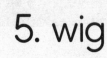

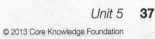

6. bib

7. yes

8. wet

9. rip

10. jug

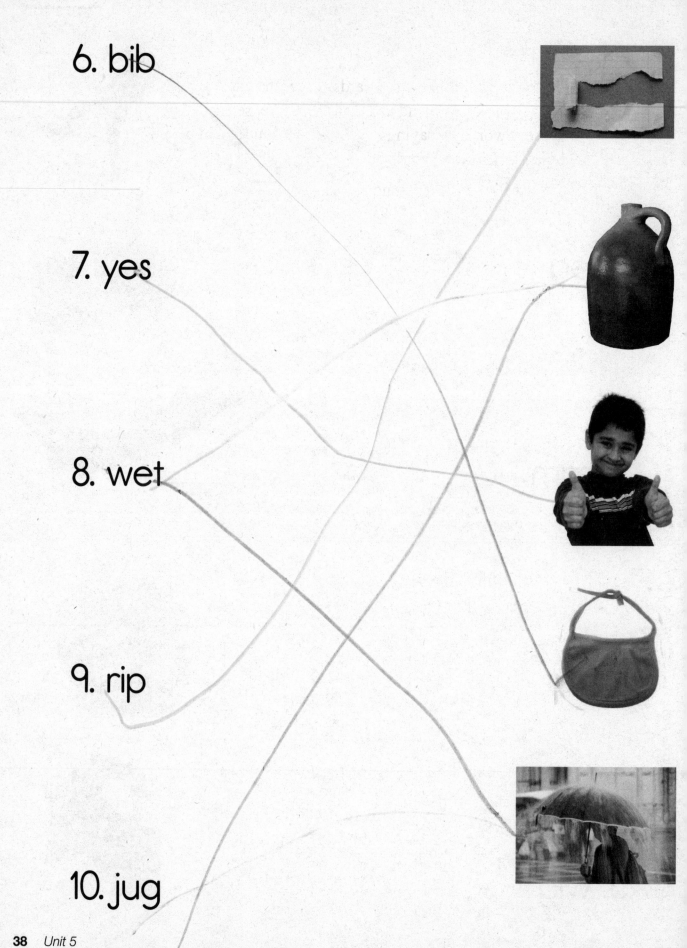

Dear Family Member,

Help your child cut out the word cards. Show the cards to your child and have your child blend and read them. Please encourage your child to read the words by saying the individual sounds and blending them together to make the word.

Extension: Read the words aloud and have your child write down the sounds, one at a time. Please keep the cards for future practice.

yes	big	win
bit	jet	run
wet	cup	lid
jam	rip	bed

Directions: Have students trace and copy the letters and words. The motion for 'x' can be described as 1. diagonal right, 2. diagonal left. Encourage students to say the sounds while writing the letters.

1. big box

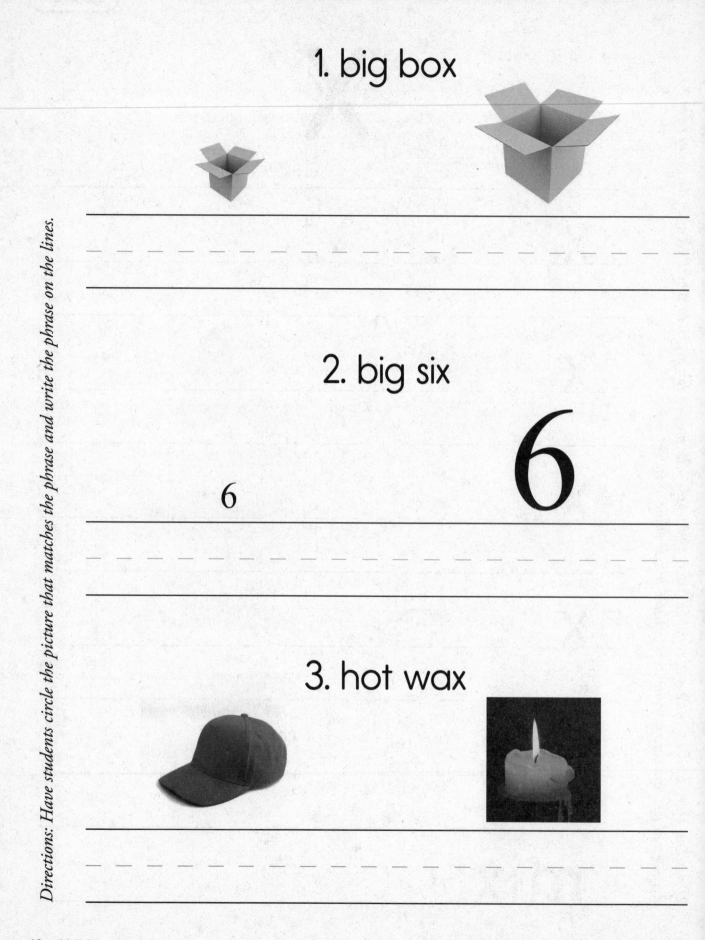

2. big six

6

6

3. hot wax

Directions: Have students circle the picture that matches the phrase and write the phrase on the lines.

Dear Family Member,

Please help your child cut out the picture cards on this page. On Worksheet 9.3 have your child glue or tape pictures beginning with the /l/ sound (log, lip, leg) under the 'l' heading. Next, glue or tape the pictures beginning with the /r/ sound (rat, ram, rug) under the 'r' heading.

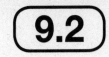

Dear Family Member,

Please have your child glue or tape the pictures from Worksheet 9.2 here. Affix pictures beginning with the /l/ sound under the 'l' heading and pictures beginning with the /r/ sound under the 'r' heading.

l | r

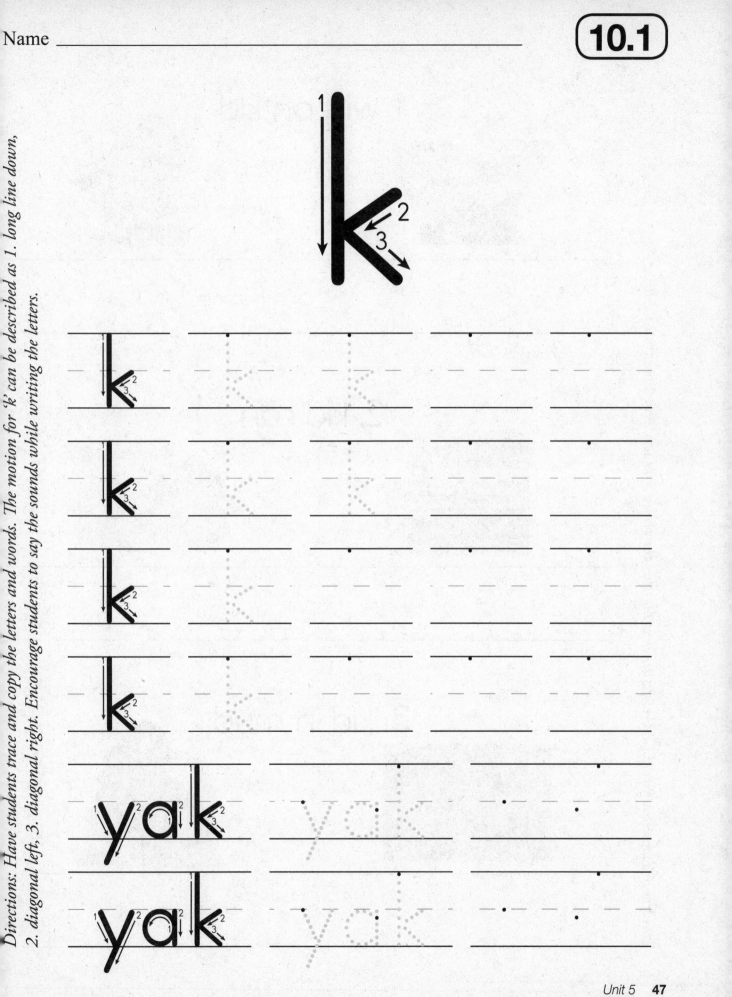

Directions: Have students trace and copy the letters and words. The motion for 'k' can be described as 1. long line down, 2. diagonal left, 3. diagonal right. Encourage students to say the sounds while writing the letters.

1. wig on kid

2. kid ran

3. kid in mud

Directions: Have students circle the picture that matches the phrase and write the phrase on the lines.

Directions: Have students write the words that begin with the /k/ sound spelled 'c' under the 'c' header and words that begin with the /k/ sound spelled 'k' under the 'k' header.

cat	cub	cot	kit	kin
cab	ken	cut	cop	kid

as in <u>c</u>up

as in <u>k</u>id

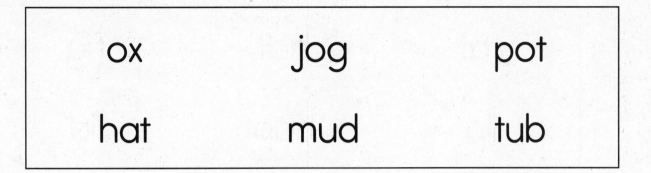

| ox | jog | pot |
| hat | mud | tub |

Directions: Have students write each word under the matching picture.

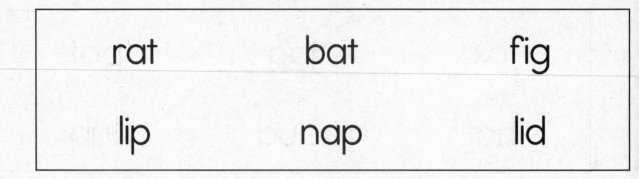

| rat | bat | fig |
| lip | nap | lid |

Directions: Have students write each word under the matching picture.

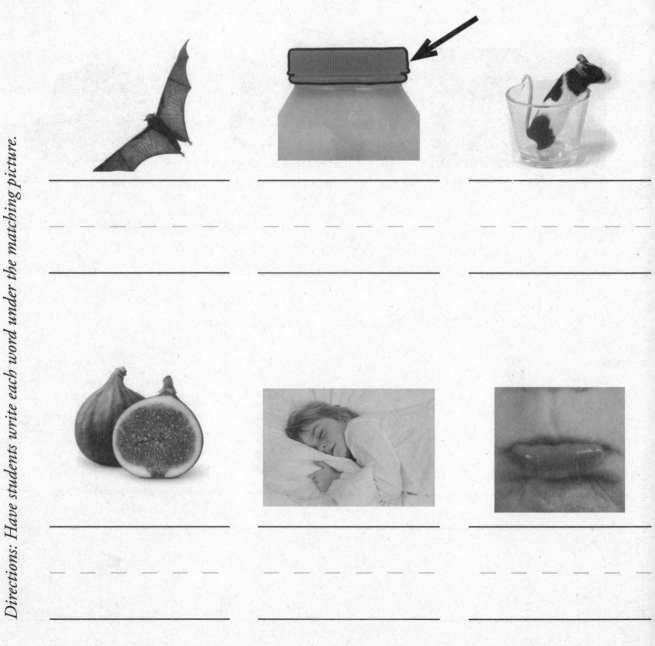

Name _____

Dear Family Member,

  On the front and back of this worksheet, have your child draw a
line from each word on the left to the matching picture. If necessary,
identify the pictures for your child.

1. yam

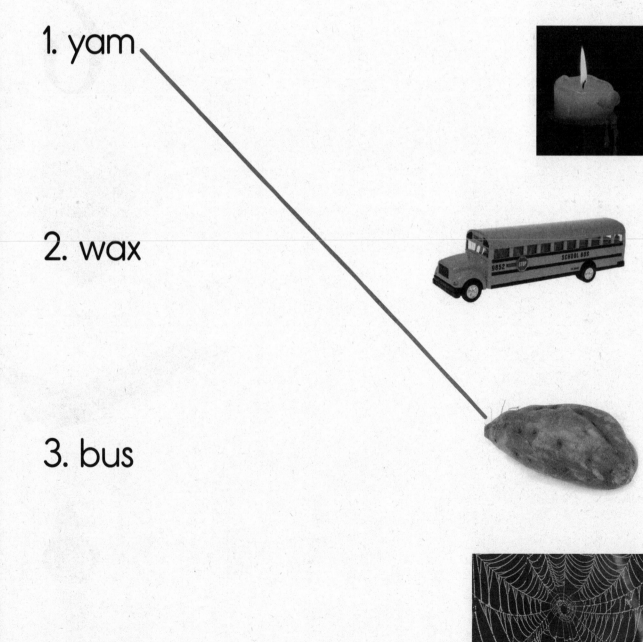

2. wax

3. bus

4. web

5. box

6. jet

7. kid

8. jam

9. six

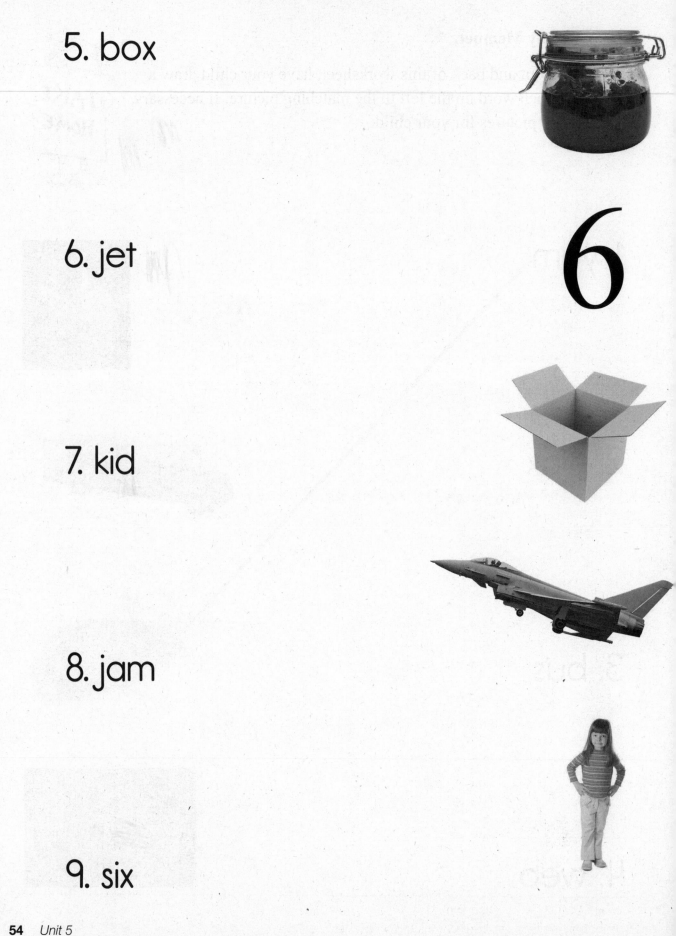

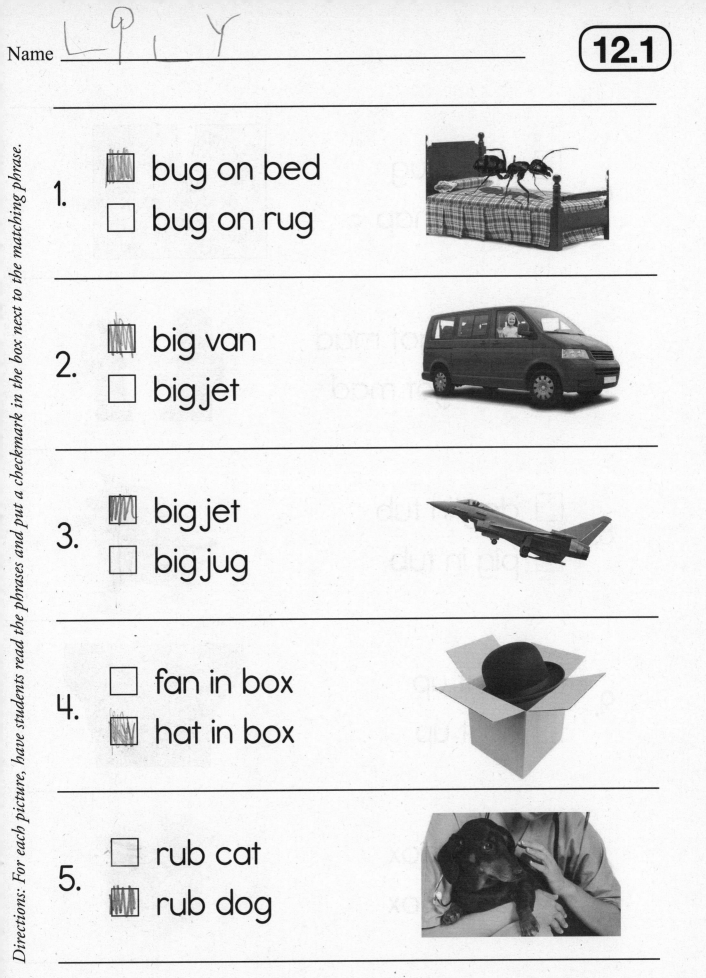

Directions: For each picture, have students read the phrases and put a checkmark in the box next to the matching phrase.

1. ☒ bug on bed
   ☐ bug on rug

2. ☒ big van
   ☐ big jet

3. ☒ big jet
   ☐ big jug

4. ☐ fan in box
   ☒ hat in box

5. ☐ rub cat
   ☒ rub dog

6. ☐ rip in rug
    ☒ rip in map

7. ☒ mom got mad
    ☐ dad got mad

8. ☐ dog in tub
    ☒ pig in tub

9. ☒ zip it up
    ☐ rip it up

10. ☐ rat in box
    ☒ fox in box

Directions: Have students trace each letter several times inside of the outline, using a different-colored crayon each time. Make sure students start tracing at the black dots.

Record Sheet for Unit 5 Word Reading

Place a check next to each word read correctly. For words that are misread, write exactly what the student says as he sounds out the word. If a student misreads a word, prompt him or her to try to read the word again.

WORD	FIRST ATTEMPT	SECOND ATTEMPT/NOTES
1. leg		
2. kid		
3. rat		
4. jug		
5. yes		
6. jet		
7. log		
8. box		
9. web		
10. rug		
TOTAL CORRECT	/30	

SUBTOTAL: _____

'l' >/l/ (1,7)____/2   'e'>/e/ (1, 5,6,9) ___/4   'g'>/g/ (1,4, 7, 10) ___/4   'k'>/k/ (1) ___/1

'i'>/i/ (2) _____/1   'd'>/d/ (2) _____/1   'r'>/r/ (3,10) ____/2   'a'>/a/ (3) ___/1

't'>/t/ (3,6) _____/2   'j'>/j/ (4,6) ____/2   'u'/>u/ (4,10) ___/2   'y'>/y/ (5) ___/1

's'>/s/ (5)___/1   'o'>/o/ (7, 8) ____/2   'b'>/b/ (8, 9)_____/2   'x'>/x/ (8)___/1

'w'>/w/ (9) _____/1

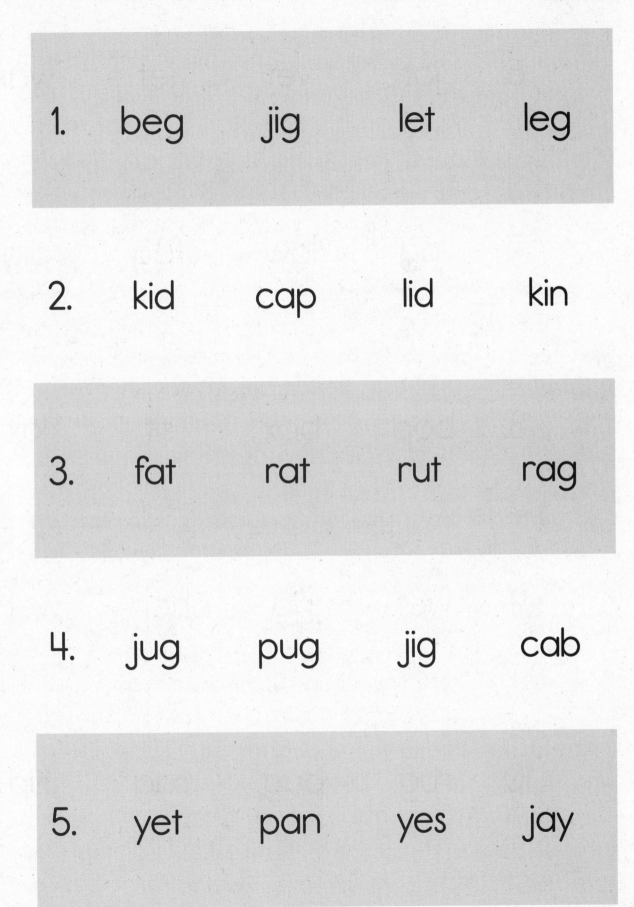

1. beg   jig   let   leg

2. kid   cap   lid   kin

3. fat   rat   rut   rag

4. jug   pug   jig   cab

5. yet   pan   yes   jay

Directions: In each row, have the students circle the word the teacher says aloud.

6. jot   yet   jet   wax

7. log   law   fog   pig

8. bop   box   sit   lox

9. wet   rib   hen   web

10. rug   bug   rag   zip

Dear Family Member,

Help your child cut out the word cards. Show the cards and have your child blend and read them. Please encourage him or her to read the words by saying the individual sounds and then blending them together to make the word.

Extension: Read the words aloud and have your child write down the sounds, one at a time. Please keep the cards for future practice.

lid	log	yet
web	tub	jet
bun	kid	job
six	rot	kin

yet	leg	lid
jet	tub	web
job	kid	bun
kin	rot	six

Name _LILY w_

box   jet   leg

wig   rug   kid

Kid   leg   jit

box   wig   boptg

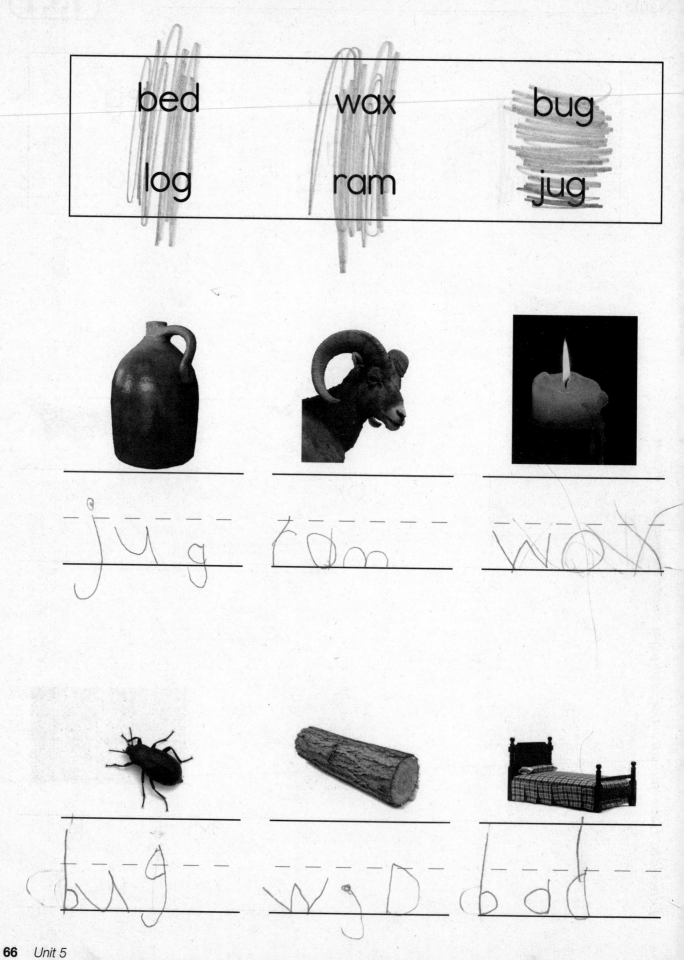

bed	wax	bug
log	ram	jug

jug

ram

wax

bug

wg

bd

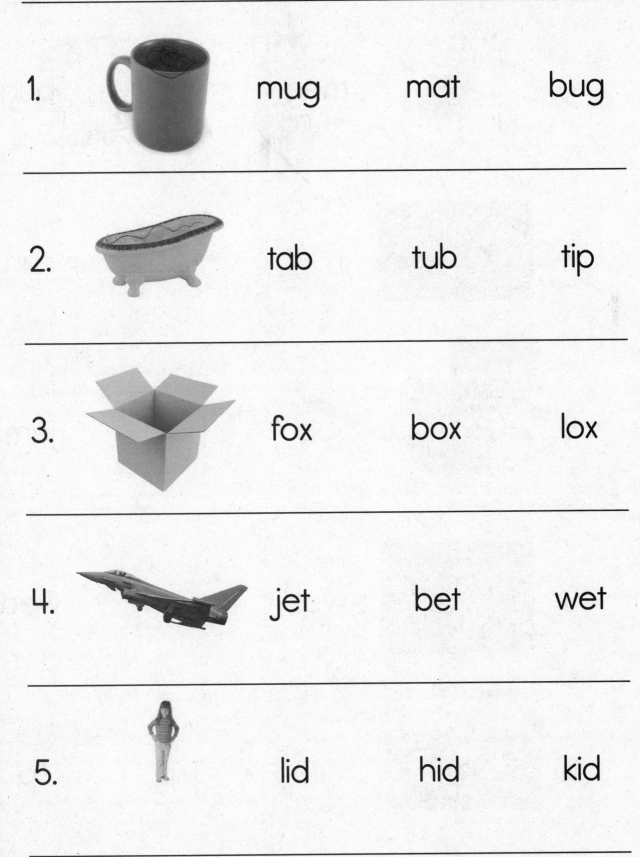

1.   mug   mat   bug

2.   tab   tub   tip

3.   fox   box   lox

4.   jet   bet   wet

5.   lid   hid   kid

Directions: For each picture, have students circle the matching word.

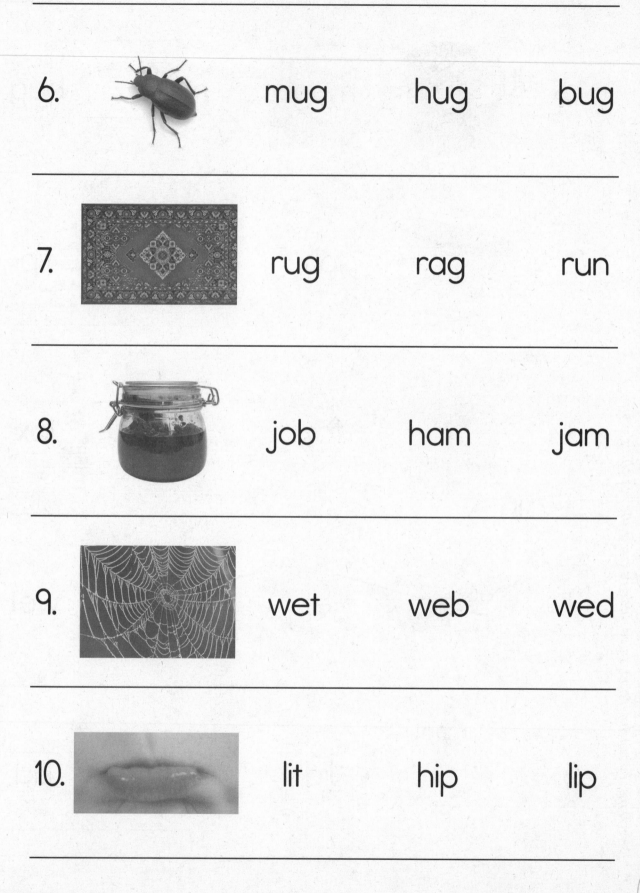

6. mug   hug   bug

7. rug   rag   run

8. job   ham   jam

9. wet   web   wed

10. lit   hip   lip

Directions: Have students circle the dictated words and copy them on the lines.

1. kit   fit

2. lip   lid

3. rat   pat

4. fin   win

5. yet   get

6. it   sit

Directions: Have students write the words that contain the /i/ sound spelled 'i' under the 'i' header and words containing the /e/ sound spelled 'e' under the 'e' header.

| wig | let | jet | bet | rip |
| fix | wet | win | yes | bin |

as in i̱t

as in we̱t

box	lot	sun	bun	cup
run	rub	pop	dot	rot

as in c<u>u</u>p

as in t<u>o</u>p

Name _____

Dear Family Member,

On the front and back of this worksheet have your child copy each word under the matching picture. If necessary, identify the pictures for your child.

1. wig

_____

- - - - - - - - - - - - - -

_____

2. jug

 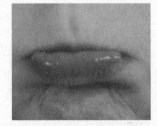

_____

- - - - - - - - - - - - - -

_____

3. box

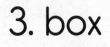 

_____

- - - - - - - - - - - - - -

_____

4. jam

jam

5. mug

mug

6. ram

ram

Name _____

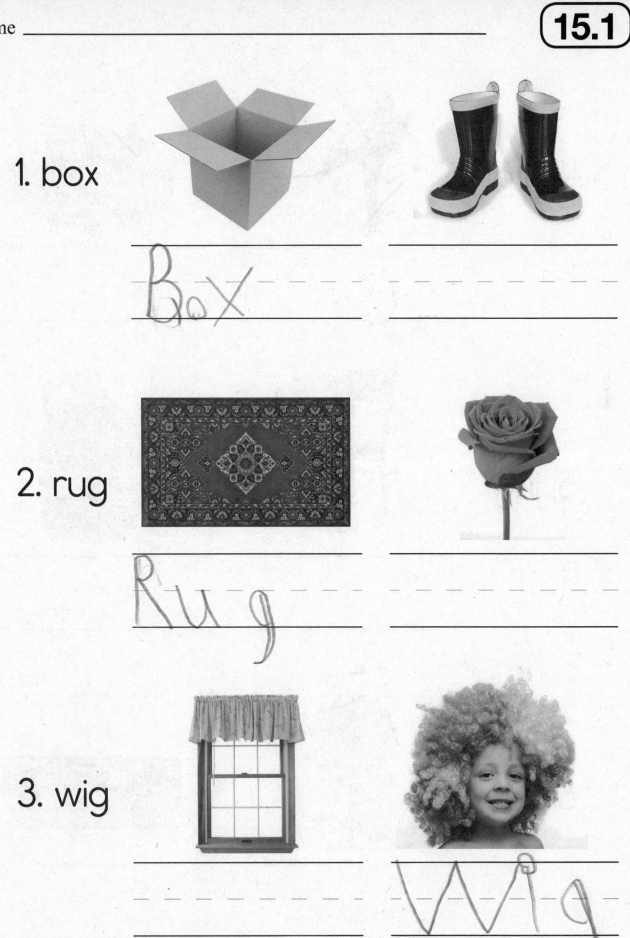

1. box

Box

2. rug

Rug

3. wig

Wig

Unit 5 77
© 2013 Core Knowledge Foundation

Directions: Have students write each word under the matching picture.

4. leg

Leg

5. jug

jug

6. lid

lid

Name _____

Directions: For each picture, have students circle the letters that spell the name of the depicted item. Students should write the name of the item on the line.

h
d

e
a

p
n

hen

c
s

u
e

n
m

sun

p
b

o
i

k
x

box

l
h

e
a

k
g

leg

b
p

u
o

z
s

bus

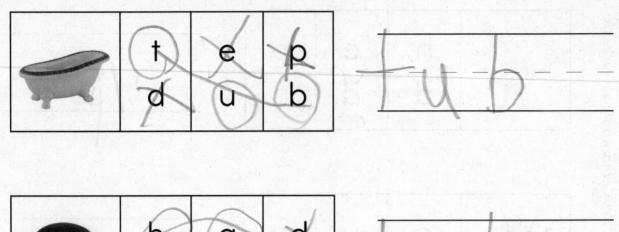

tub

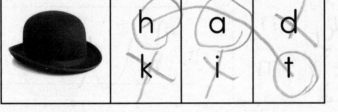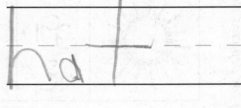

hat

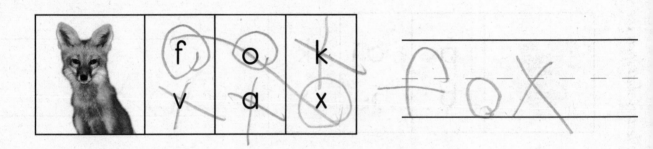

fox

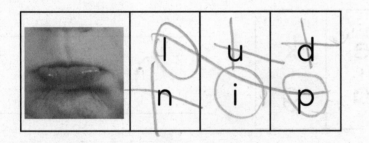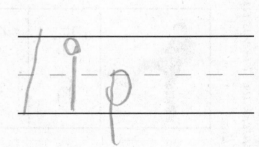

lip

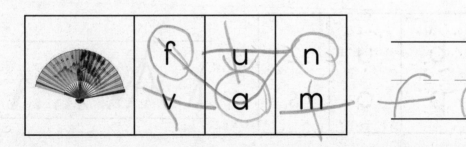

fan

Directions: For each picture, have students read the phrases and put a checkmark in the box next to the matching phrase.

1. ☐ rat in cup
   ☐ rat in hat

2. ☐ jug in bag
   ☐ bag on bed

3. ☐ ant on bat
   ☐ ant on bed

4. ☐ pup in tub
   ☐ fox in tub

5. ☐ kid in mud
   ☐ pig in mud

6. ☐ fox in box
   ☐ fox on box

7. ☐ bug in tub
   ☐ bug on rug

8. ☐ kid in mud
   ☐ kid in tub

9. ☐ hug mom
   ☐ hug dog

10. ☐ dog in sun
    ☐ cat in sun

Directions: Have students hold up this worksheet when you say /p/.

_____

Directions: Have students hold up this worksheet when you say /b/.

_____

Name _____

PP3

Directions: Have students hold up this worksheet when you say /t/.

Name _____

Directions: Have students hold up this worksheet when you say /d/.

_____

Name _____

Directions: Have students hold up this worksheet when you say /k/.

Directions: Have students hold up this worksheet when you say /g/.

Name _____

Directions: Have students hold up this worksheet when you say /f/.

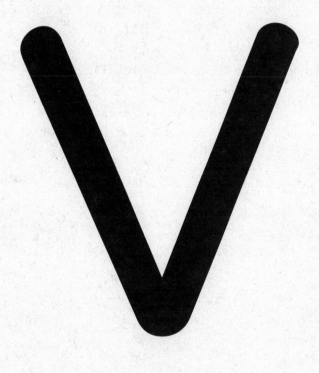

Directions: Have students hold up this worksheet when you say /v/.

Directions: Have students hold up this worksheet when you say /s/.

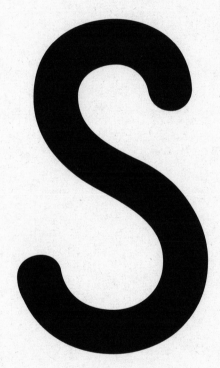

Name _____

Directions: Have students hold up this worksheet when you say /z/.

cup	ask	elk	kin	cod
doc	cap	kit	cab	kid

as in <u>c</u>at

_____

- - - - - - - - - - - - - - -

_____

- - - - - - - - - - - - - - -

_____

- - - - - - - - - - - - - - -

_____

- - - - - - - - - - - - - - -

_____

- - - - - - - - - - - - - - -

_____

as in <u>k</u>it

_____

- - - - - - - - - - - - - - -

_____

- - - - - - - - - - - - - - -

_____

- - - - - - - - - - - - - - -

_____

- - - - - - - - - - - - - - -

_____

- - - - - - - - - - - - - - -

_____

Directions: Have students write the words with the /k/ sound spelled 'c' under the 'c' header and words with the /k/ sound spelled 'k' under the 'k' header.

Directions: Have students cut out the word cards and place them on the matching words on Worksheet PP13.

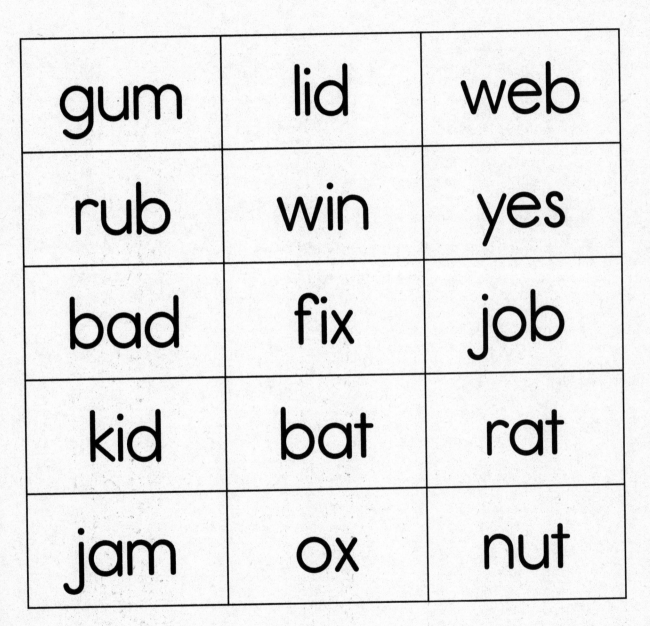

gum	lid	web
rub	win	yes
bad	fix	job
kid	bat	rat
jam	ox	nut

Name

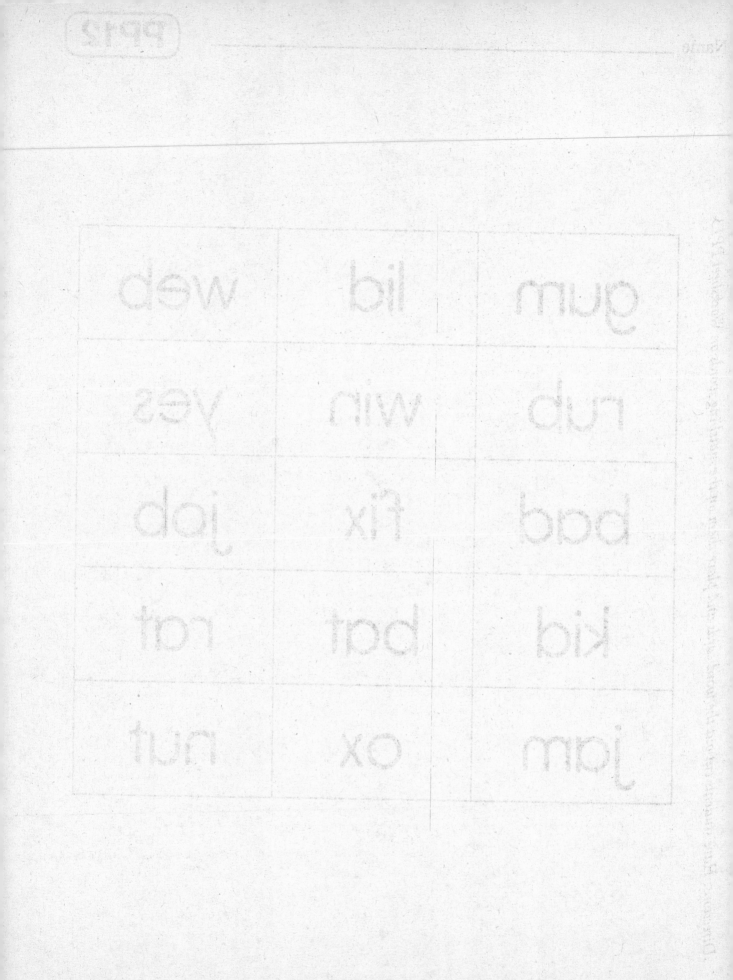

web	lid	gum
yes	win	rub
job	fix	bad
rat	bat	kid
nut	ox	jam

Directions: Have students read the word cards from Worksheet PP12 and place them on the matching words on this worksheet.

bad	yes	win
fix	job	rub
kid	bat	web
jam	rat	lid
ox	nut	gum

Directions: Have students trace and copy the letters. Encourage students to say the sounds while writing the letters.

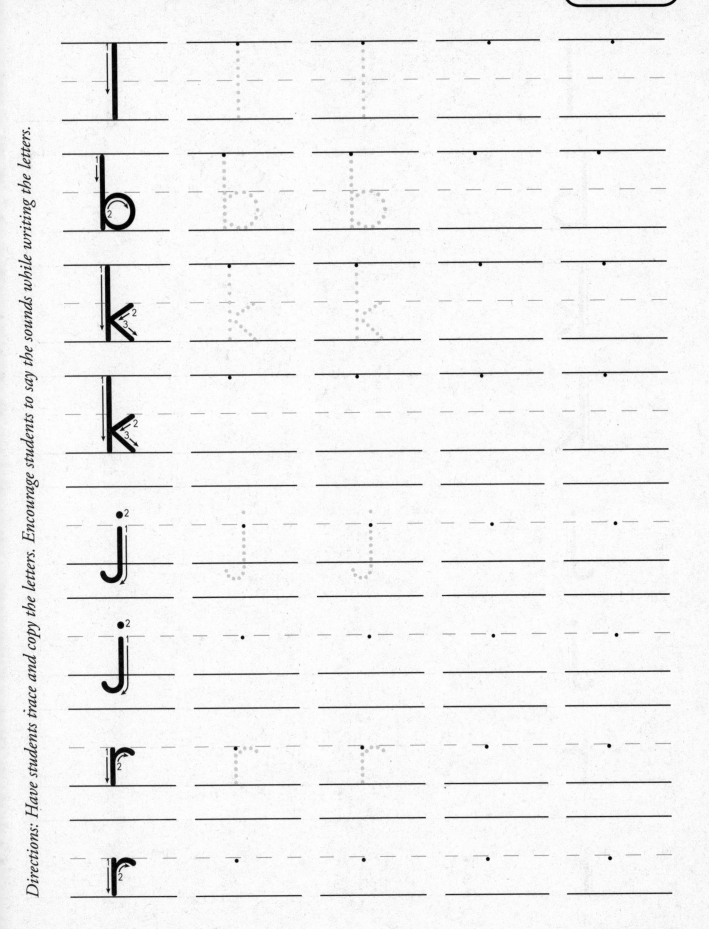

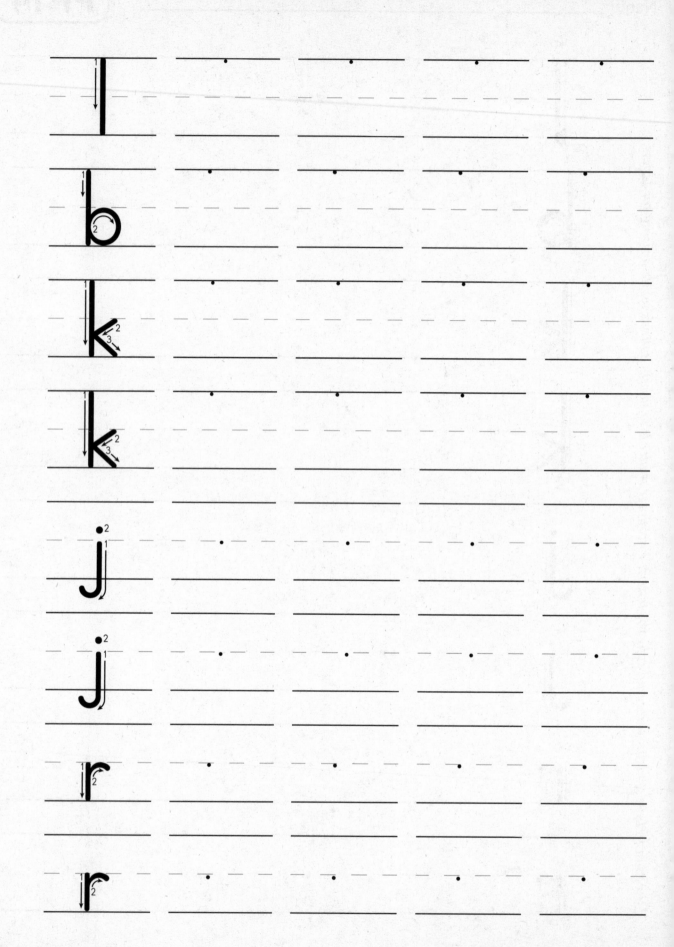

Directions: Have students trace and copy the letters. Encourage students to say the sounds while writing each letter.

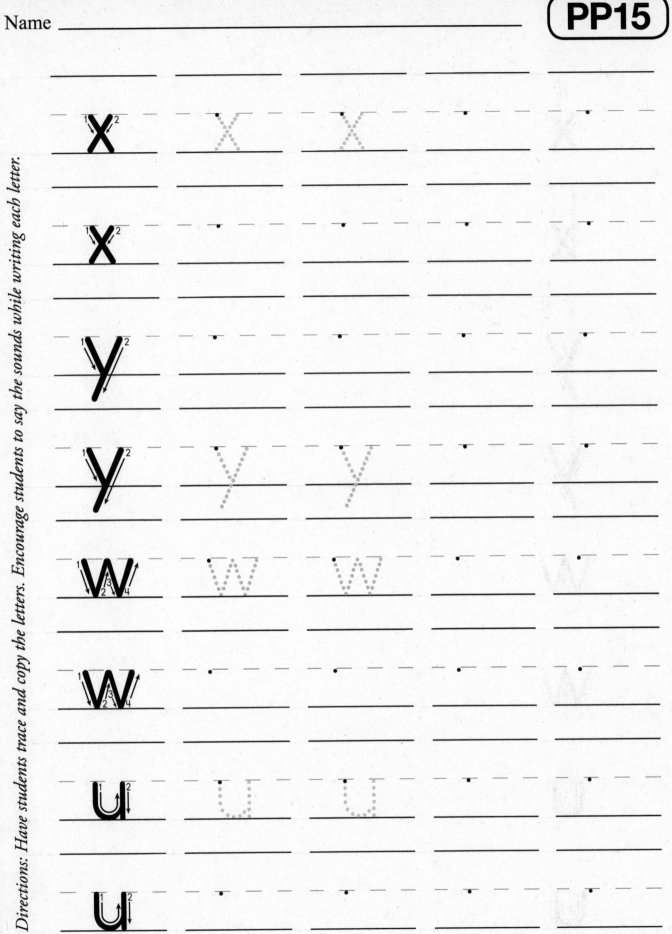

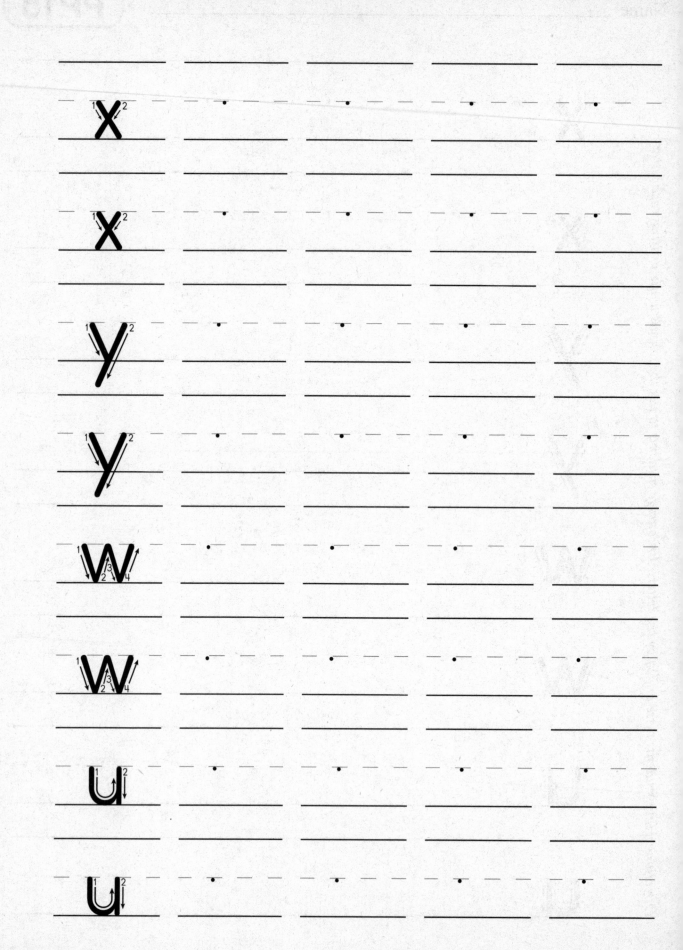

Directions: Have students trace and copy the words. Encourage students to say the sounds while writing each letter.

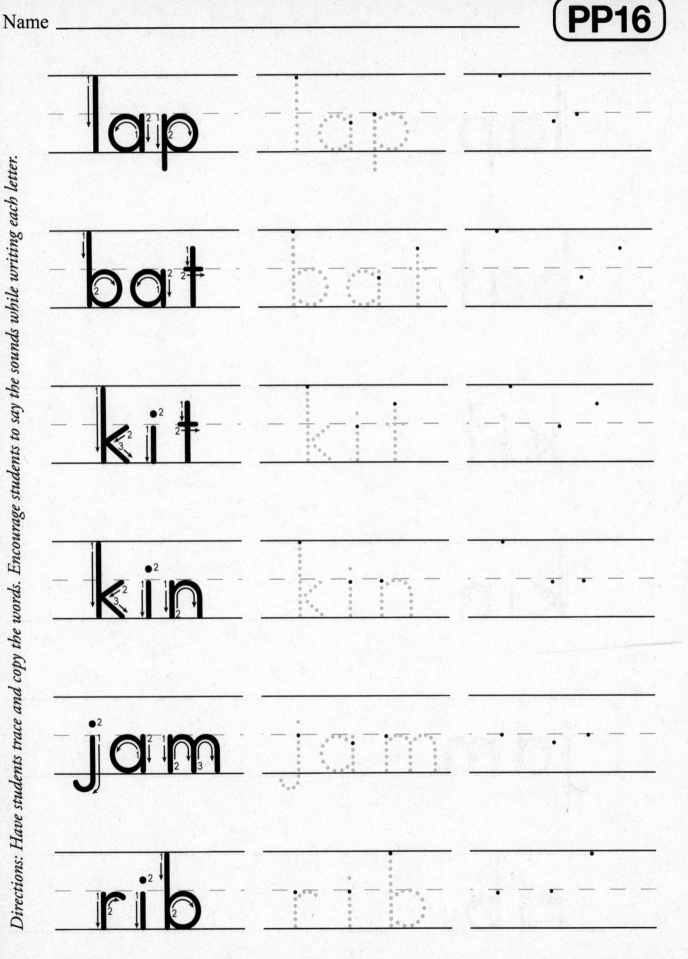

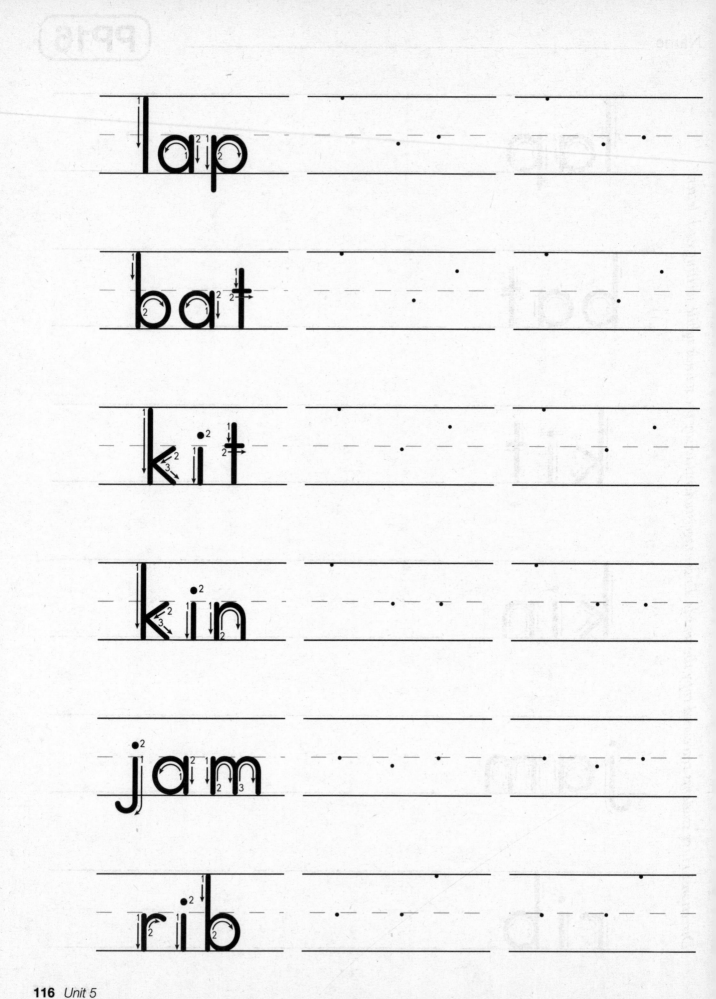

Directions: Have students trace and copy the words. Encourage students to say the sounds while writing each letter.

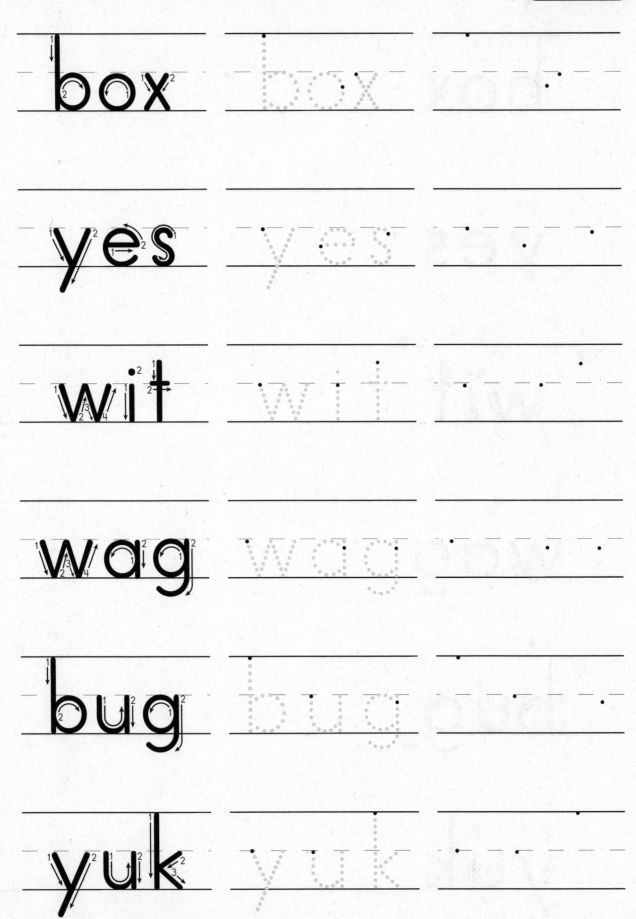

box

yes

wit

wag

bug

yuk

box

yes

wit

wag

bug

yuk

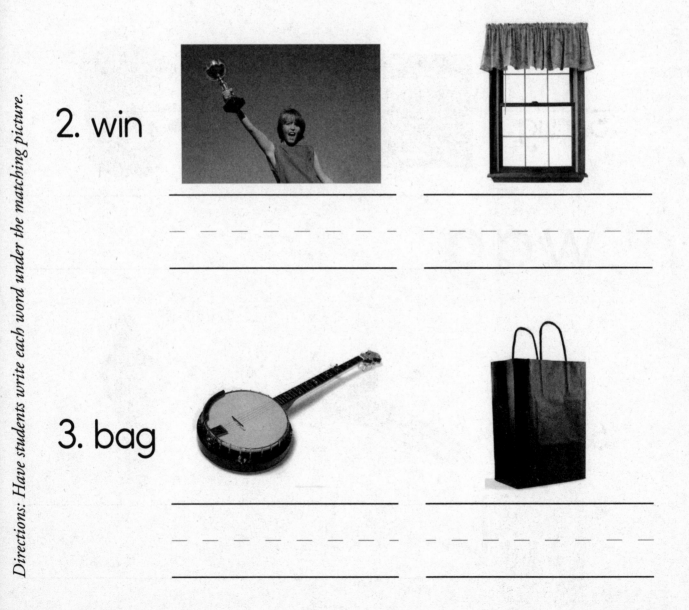

Directions: Have students write each word under the matching picture.

1. jam

2. win

3. bag

4. box

_____

- - - - - - - - - - - -

_____

5. rug

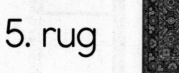

_____

- - - - - - - - - - - -

_____

6. kid

_____

- - - - - - - - - - - -

_____

Directions: Have students write each word under the matching picture.

jet	box	run
kid	wax	lip

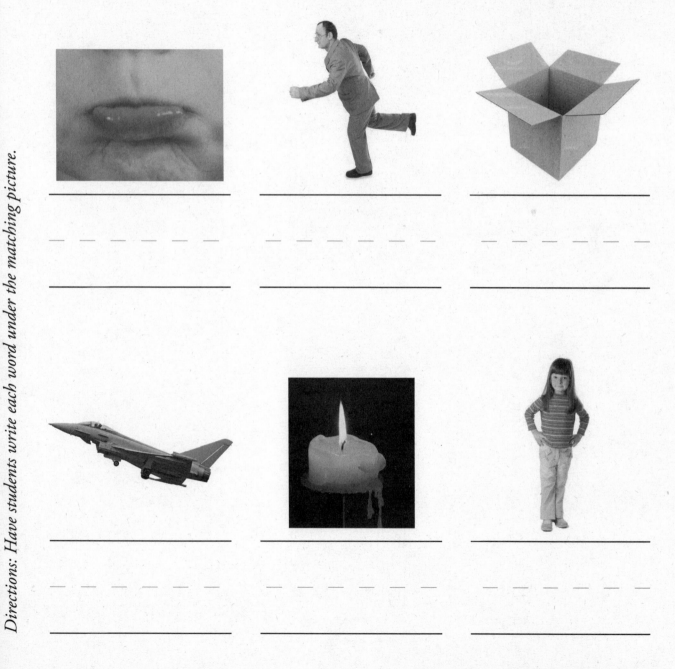

hip   net   bit   him   wed

sit   let   win   hen   red

Directions: Have students write the words with the /i/ sound spelled 'i' under the 'i' header and words with the /e/ sound spelled 'e' under the 'e' header.

as in i̲t

as in we̲t

| cab | cup | hat | bus | sad |
| sun | tan | pug | tub | jam |

Directions: Have students write the words with the /u/ sound spelled 'u' under the 'u' header and words with the /a/ sound spelled 'a' under the 'a' header.

as in r<u>u</u>b

_____

- - - - - - - - -

_____

- - - - - - - - -

_____

- - - - - - - - -

_____

_____

- - - - - - - - -

_____

- - - - - - - - -

_____

as in r<u>a</u>t

_____

- - - - - - - - -

_____

- - - - - - - - -

_____

- - - - - - - - -

_____

_____

- - - - - - - - -

_____

- - - - - - - - -

_____

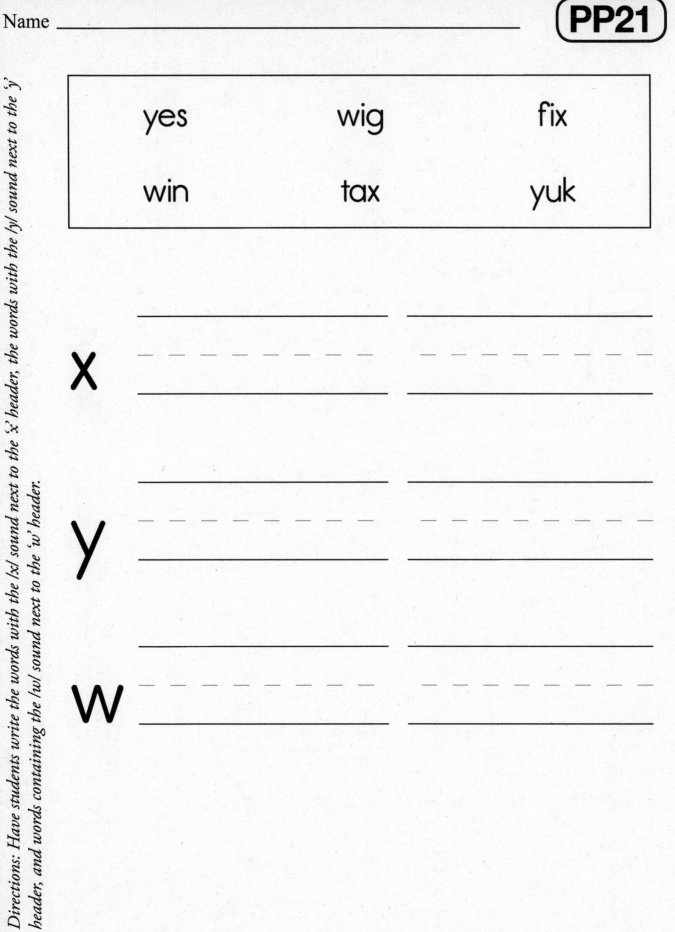

CORE KNOWLEDGE LANGUAGE ARTS

SERIES EDITOR-IN-CHIEF
E. D. Hirsch, Jr.

PRESIDENT
Linda Bevilacqua

EDITORIAL STAFF
Carolyn Gosse, Senior Editor - Preschool
Khara Turnbull, Materials Development Manager
Michelle L. Warner, Senior Editor - Listening & Learning

Mick Anderson
Robin Blackshire
Maggie Buchanan
Paula Coyner
Sue Fulton
Sara Hunt
Erin Kist
Robin Luecke
Rosie McCormick
Cynthia Peng
Liz Pettit
Ellen Sadler
Deborah Samley
Diane Auger Smith
Sarah Zelinke

DESIGN AND GRAPHICS STAFF
Scott Ritchie, Creative Director

Kim Berrall
Michael Donegan
Liza Greene
Matt Leech
Bridget Moriarty
Lauren Pack

CONSULTING PROJECT MANAGEMENT SERVICES
ScribeConcepts.com

ADDITIONAL CONSULTING SERVICES
Ang Blanchette
Dorrit Green
Carolyn Pinkerton

ACKNOWLEDGMENTS

These materials are the result of the work, advice, and encouragement of numerous individuals over many years. Some of those singled out here already know the depth of our gratitude; others may be surprised to find themselves thanked publicly for help they gave quietly and generously for the sake of the enterprise alone. To helpers named and unnamed we are deeply grateful.

CONTRIBUTORS TO EARLIER VERSIONS OF THESE MATERIALS
Susan B. Albaugh, Kazuko Ashizawa, Nancy Braier, Kathryn M. Cummings, Michelle De Groot, Diana Espinal, Mary E. Forbes, Michael L. Ford, Ted Hirsch, Danielle Knecht, James K. Lee, Diane Henry Leipzig, Martha G. Mack, Liana Mahoney, Isabel McLean, Steve Morrison, Juliane K. Munson, Elizabeth B. Rasmussen, Laura Tortorelli, Rachael L. Shaw, Sivan B. Sherman, Miriam E. Vidaver, Catherine S. Whittington, Jeannette A. Williams

We would like to extend special recognition to Program Directors Matthew Davis and Souzanne Wright who were instrumental to the early development of this program.

SCHOOLS
We are truly grateful to the teachers, students, and administrators of the following schools for their willingness to field test these materials and for their invaluable advice: Capitol View Elementary, Challenge Foundation Academy (IN), Community Academy Public Charter School, Lake Lure Classical Academy, Lepanto Elementary School, New Holland Core Knowledge Academy, Paramount School of Excellence, Pioneer Challenge Foundation Academy, New York City PS 26R (The Carteret School), PS 30X (Wilton School), PS 50X (Clara Barton School), PS 96Q, PS 102X (Joseph O. Loretan), PS 104Q (The Bays Water), PS 214K (Michael Friedsam), PS 223Q (Lyndon B. Johnson School), PS 308K (Clara Cardwell), PS 333Q (Goldie Maple Academy), Sequoyah Elementary School, South Shore Charter Public School, Spartanburg Charter School, Steed Elementary School, Thomas Jefferson Classical Academy, Three Oaks Elementary, West Manor Elementary.

And a special thanks to the CKLA Pilot Coordinators Anita Henderson, Yasmin Lugo-Hernandez, and Susan Smith, whose suggestions and day-to-day support to teachers using these materials in their classrooms was critical.

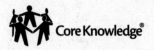

CREDITS

ILLUSTRATORS AND IMAGE SOURCES

Cover: Shutterstock; Title Page: Shutterstock; Take Home Icon: Core Knowledge Staff; 1.1: Shutterstock; 1.2: Shutterstock; 2.1: Shutterstock; 3.1: Shutterstock; 3.2: Shutterstock; 4.1: Shutterstock; 5.1: Shutterstock; 5.2: Shutterstock; 5.3: Shutterstock; 6.1: Shutterstock; 6.2: Shutterstock; 7.1: Shutterstock; 7.2: Shutterstock; 8.1: Shutterstock; 8.2: Shutterstock; 8.3: Shutterstock; 9.1: Shutterstock; 9.2: Shutterstock; 10.1: Shutterstock; 11.1: Shutterstock; 11.1 (ox): Jed Henry; 11.2: Shutterstock; 12.1: Shutterstock; 13.1: Shutterstock; 13.2: Shutterstock; 14.2: Shutterstock; 14.4: Shutterstock; 15.1: Shutterstock; 15.2: Shutterstock; 16.1: Shutterstock; 16.2: Jed Henry; PP18: Shutterstock; PP19: Shutterstock